# CATS are cheaper than THERAPY

# CATS are cheaper than THERAPY

LIFE ADVICE FROM FELINE EXPURRTS

Andrews McMeel
PUBLISHING®

Cats are expurrts at taking care of themselves. They take frequent naps to rest and recharge, embrace playfulness, follow strict fur-care routines, and even set boundaries with those around them. To put it simply, we frazzled humans could learn a thing or two from our kitty companions. So sit back, relax, and take in the charming purrspectives of these whiskered wellness experts . . .

Don't let your one
and only life flutter by.
Follow your pawssions!

Sometimes you just
gotta fake a smile.

If you're looking for
a spiritual practice,
I recommend pillow yoga.
It's also good if you snore.

Take time to eat.
Nobody wants to see
you hangry, no matter
how cute you are.

Go ahead. It's okay to
let your felines out.

Relaxing with a buddy makes for a purrfect day.

If you want to open up
and share your feelings,
I'm all ears.

Eating can be a mindful
time of togetherness.
Just keep your kibbles
to yourself.

Find a sunny spot and spread out.
Maybe someone will take notice
and give you a tummy scratch.

When on the fence about a direction in life, always choose the side that puts food in a bowl.

Try to look at things from diffurent purrspectives.

I'm good enough,
I'm smart enough, and
doggone it, I couldn't care
less if people like me.

Feeling vulnerable?
Fetal pawsition to
the rescue!

Taking on too much can be jarring to your system.

Self-Care 101:
The power of a good sleep
is immeowsurable.

Sometimes you just
gotta tell yourself,
"I'm pawsome!"

To meditate, clear your mind of all thoughts. Easy for me—there's not a lot going on up there anyway.

Engage in relaxing
purrsuits every day.

Peek-a-boo! I see you!
Make time to play
every day.

Some days the best therapy is to hide!

If it seems like
everything is upside down
in life, roll over.

Never underestimate the pawer of thinking pawsitively.

Exercising outdoors relieves stress. I recommend chasing birds.

I'm an optimist.
I choose to see the
food dish as half-full.

We're all treemendous and purrfect in our own special ways.

After a spat, it's good
to hiss and make up.

Reflecting on the past
can keep you stuck.
Live for the meow!

Practice humility.
Or cuteness.
Whichever's easier.

The world can be
a scary place.
Sometimes you've
just got to take it
lying down. For a nap.

Taking in the sounds
and smells of nature will
leave you feline fine.

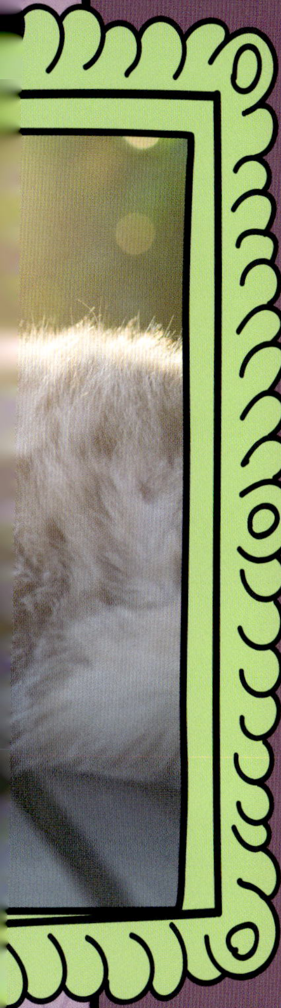

It's good for your mental health to wake up with the sun. I think that's around noonish?

A good furiend is purrfect to lean on.

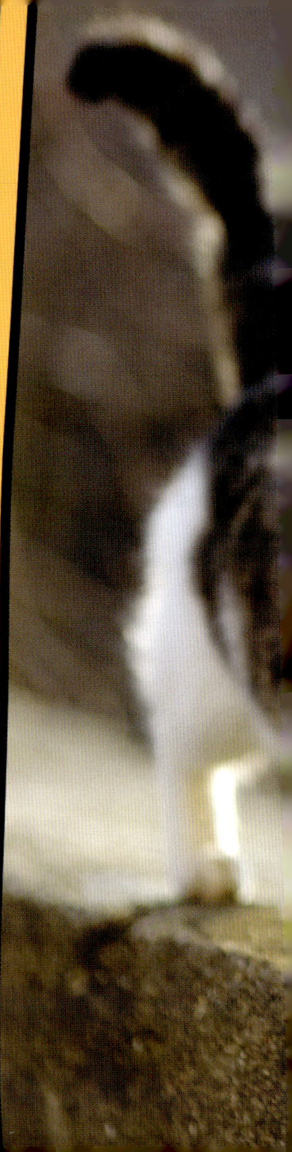

Hiding from the pawblem
ain't gonna fix it.

Have the courage to log off and follow your own path.

You can still have a
good day, even if you
wake up with bed ears.

My Advice:
A mind is like a door.
Try to keep it open.

Comfort is its own reward.

Even for introverts, getting out of the house can be a pawsitive change of scenery.

Nothing beats a good scream to release some tension.

Some days you're just
beside yourself.

Reaching out and
asking for help can
be uncomfurtable, but
it's one of the bravest
things you can do.

Being someplace cozy
is my cup of tea.

I've never climbed a tree before, but I'm branching out.

A bouquet can
purrk up your day.

Everyone has something to bring to the table. I hope what you bring tastes like chicken.

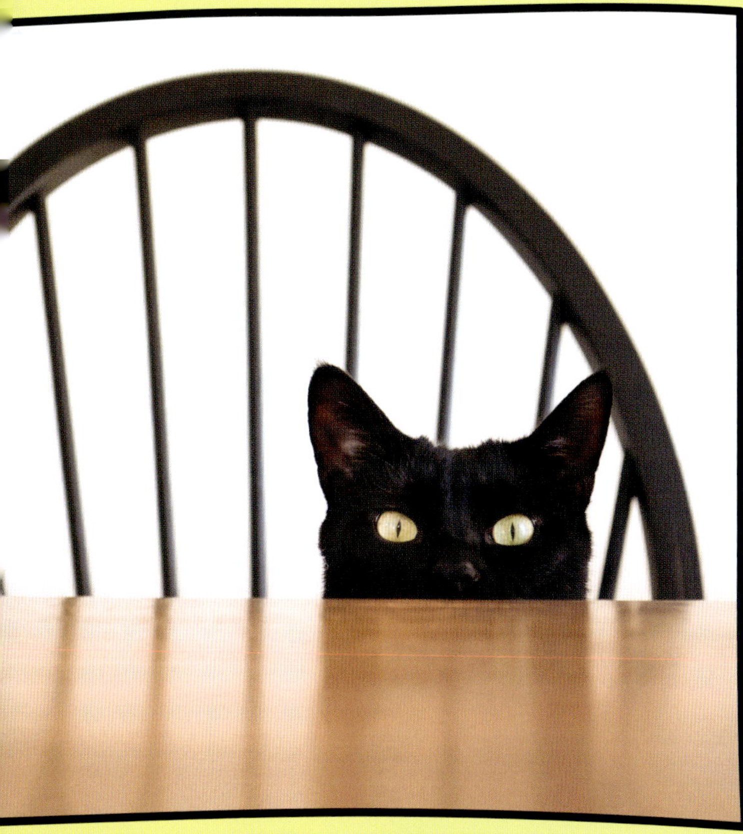

I recommend couch therapy. From midmorning nap to suppertime.

Apprehensive about
what's around the bend?
Trust good furiends to
have your back.

Daily affurmation:
I am beautiful, yes,
but I'm also more than
just a purrty face.

Be open to what life hands you. Just remember to blink.

Hanging with a bestie
is therapawtic.

Self-Help 101:
No purrcrastinating—jump on what needs to be done!

Take a break from
life's furantic pace.
Make time for a catnap.

The rest of your life
starts right meow!

The authorised representative in the EEA is Simon and Schuster Netherlands BV, Herculesplein 96 3584 AA Utrecht, Netherlands. (info@simonandschuster.nl)

Andrews McMeel Publishing
a division of Andrews McMeel Universal
1130 Walnut Street, Kansas City, Missouri 64106

www.andrewsmcmeel.com

25 26 27 28 29 TEN 10 9 8 7 6 5 4 3 2 1

ISBN: 979-8-8816-0495-0

Library of Congress Control Number: 2025932634



Text by Eric Scott, Charlie Colborne, and Sarah Tobaben

Editor: Erin Renk
Art Director: Abby Gust Hutter
Production Editor: Kayla Overbey
Production Manager: Tamara Haus

FSC
www.fsc.org
MIX
Paper | Supporting responsible forestry
FSC® C016973

**ATTENTION: SCHOOLS AND BUSINESSES**
Andrews McMeel books are available at quantity discounts with bulk purchase for educational, business, or sales promotional use. For information, please email the Andrews McMeel Publishing Special Sales Department: sales@andrewsmcmeel.com.